Contents

■

see what sin does to relationships

■

identify and reflect on experiences of sin, alienation, forgiveness, and reconciliation

■

understand the role of God's love in forgiveness

■

develop an appreciation of the sacrament of Penance as the Church's celebration of forgiveness

■

How To Use This Book

Forgiveness and Healing offers the components—from icebreakers to prayer experiences— needed for a complete three-hour session. You'll find engaging activities to help you share Church teaching with teens in an effective and meaningful way, as well as doctrinal and scriptural background to help you feel comfortable with the topic. The flexible format gives you the freedom to select components that fit your time frame, teaching style, and the interest of the teens you are working with. For your convenience, each component is listed in ***Contents***, page 1, with a suggestion for approximately how long its presentation will take.

Options

Small-group setting (up to twelve participants)

Meet with the group in as comfortable and intimate a setting as possible—a carpeted conference or meeting room, or a large room in a home. If the group is meeting in a classroom, try to minimize the school atmosphere.

Large-group setting (more than twelve participants)

Young persons are sometimes uncomfortable speaking up in front of a large group. So if there will be more than twelve participants, ask teens to form groups of six to eight. Each group should have a catechist, peer minister, or adult volunteer who is prepared to lead the activities and questions.

Program leaders may form small groups ahead of time from the list of participants, making sure that each group will have at least one person who is likely to keep the group on task. Participants can learn what group they are in from posted sign-in sheets, one for each group. Or different colors or symbols on nametags may indicate different groups.

Groups may also be formed as participants arrive, determined by such things as colors or styles of clothing, birthday months, favorite foods.

Discussion Helps

1

Encourage sharing by offering experiences and examples of your own.

2

Be appreciative of honest sharing. Accept every contribution with respect, even those that seem to be off the topic or difficult to understand. Sometimes gentle questioning may reveal the point the young person is making.

3

If young people seem reluctant to share in a group, allow them to write down their feelings and insights. Ask them to read what they have written, or collect and read their responses, perhaps without revealing the identities of the writers.

4

Encourage everyone to participate. It may occasionally be necessary to say to someone, "We haven't heard from you. We'd like to. What do you think about...?"

5

Encourage discussion by using these or similar statements and questions.

- That's interesting. What makes you feel this way?
- I'm sure that many of us share that feeling. Could you explain it a little more, please?
- That really helps me understand my own experience.
- Does everyone understand that?
- I'm not sure I really follow that. Could you please be more specific?

6

Be flexible. Teens may need to spend more time than planned on certain parts of the session, or they may need to discuss areas not covered in the session. Be sensitive to their questions, struggles, and concerns.

For Group Leaders

Forgiveness and Healing looks at reconciliation as a basic human need. Everyone who is alive and lives in relationship with God and other human beings experiences sin, alienation, and the need for forgiveness.

But because of God's unconditional love for us, we can also experience forgiveness. The message of the Old Testament to the chosen people is that God, a loving Father, loves them no matter what. Again and again, they receive the assurance of his forgiveness.

I will heal their disloyalty;
I will love them freely,
for my anger has turned from them.

Hosea 14:4

God's mercy and love are also primary themes in the Gospels. Jesus tells his followers about God's unconditional love and mercy in the parable of the prodigal son (Luke 15:11-32). He shows his own unconditional love and forgiveness in his meeting with Zacchaeus (Luke 19:1-10), in the stories of the sinful woman (Luke 7:36-50) and of the woman caught in adultery (John 8:1-11), and at his own crucifixion (Luke 23:32-34).

Jesus explains his choice of friends to the Pharisees by saying, "...I have come to call not the righteous but sinners (Matthew 9:13). He reminds his disciples about what the Scriptures say about him: "...it is written, that the Messiah is to suffer and to rise from the dead on the third day, and that repentance and forgiveness of sins is to be proclaimed in his name..." (Luke 24:46-47). Finally, Jesus passes his ministry of forgiveness to his disciples.

Jesus said to them again, "Peace be with you. As the Father has sent me, so I send you." When he had said this, he breathed on them and said to them, "Receive the Holy Spirit. If you forgive the sins of any, they are forgiven them; if you retain the sins of any, they are retained."

John 20:21-23

The Church, guided by the Holy Spirit, accepted its mission to forgive sins. The *Catechism of the Catholic Church* tells us that Baptism is the first sacrament by which our sins are forgiven because "it unites us to Christ , who died and rose, and gives us the Holy Spirit (*CCC,* article 985). But while Baptism cleanses us of sin, it does not change our nature. We experience weakness, and we participate in the evil in the world, even when we desire to do otherwise. Saint Paul talks about this conflict:

So I find it to be a law that when I want to do what is good, evil lies close at hand. For I delight in the law of God in my inmost self, but I see in my members another law at war with the law of my mind, making me captive to the law of sin that dwells in my members.

Romans 7:21-23

It is through the sacrament of Penance that we experience healing and wholeness in our relationships with God and others. It is precisely for this reason that the sacrament can be especially meaningful and helpful for teenagers. Young people are acutely aware of their relationships with others. At the same time they are working to establish their own identities (their relationships with themselves), they are also redefining many of their existing relationships—with parents, brothers and sisters, relatives, friends— and building new relationships—with girlfriends, boyfriends, bosses, coworkers. Relationships are very important to teens. *Forgiveness and Healing* will help you show teenagers how experiencing Gods' love and forgiveness in the sacrament of Penance can help them build, maintain, and repair their own relationships.

From the Catechism

Most of us have difficulty admitting that we have done something wrong. This common human problem often keeps people from reconciling with one another. It also keeps them from approaching the sacrament of Penance because they fear confessing their sins to a priest. The *Catechism of the Catholic Church* has an important message for us about our fears.

> The confession (or disclosure) of sins, even from a simply human point of view, frees us and facilitates our reconciliation with others. Through such an admission [one] looks squarely at the sins [one] is guilty of, takes responsibility for them, and thereby opens [oneself] again to God and to the communion of the Church in order to make a new future possible.
>
> *Catechism of the Catholic Church*, paragraph 1455

This is good news for everyone, but especially for teenagers because they are often just learning how to handle relationships. From a purely human point of view, the best way to deal with wrongdoing is to admit that we have done something wrong, say we are sorry, take responsibility for our action, try to repair any hurt or damage that has been done, and promise to try not to make the same mistake again. We can demonstrate how well the Church understands and serves human beings by pointing out that the sacrament of Penance asks us to take these steps. The penitent's acts in the sacrament are repentance (also called contrition), confession, and the intention to make reparation.

Teens can also readily understand the importance of talking about their problems. They already do this endlessly with their friends. This is another element that they can find in the way the sacrament of Penance is celebrated today. When face-to-face confession is approached with a positive attitude, the priest/ confessor is able to provide important guidance.

Icebreakers

Icebreaker 1: Welcome .... 5 minutes

Supplies • nametags • marking pens

Provide teens with a warm greeting so that they will know that you and any other group leaders participating are glad to be spending time with them.

- Wear your own nametag and have other preparations done so that you can be ready to pay attention to teens as they arrive.
- Encourage teens to fill out and put on their nametags.
- Greet each teen with a firm handshake, using the teen's name whenever possible.
- Give teens a chance to socialize and connect with one another.
- If there will be more than twelve teens participating, form small groups. See ***Options, Large-group setting***, page 2.

Icebreaker 2: Handshake of Peace Introductions .... 10 minutes

Help group members get to know one another. Form a circle or circles, depending on the size of the group. (If *Forgiveness and Healing* is being used in a large-group setting, teens can form circles in the groups they have already formed. It would be ideal if the group leader or leaders joined the circle and participated along with teens.) Ask every other participant to turn to the person on his or her right, firmly shake that person's hand, and interview the person to learn basic information about the person. After one minute, ask the interview partners to shake hands again and reverse roles. After another minute, go around the circle, asking everyone to introduce the person he or she has interviewed.

Icebreaker 3: Bible Forgiveness Figures........................ 15 minutes

Supplies • several Bibles • enough copies of ***Handout 1*** *so that each participant will have one description • tape*

Copy and cut apart ***Handout 1***. With teens standing in a circle and facing into the circle, tape one description on each person's back. Explain that you have just taped to their backs descriptions of characters from forgiveness stories from the Bible. Ask each person to find a partner who will read the description on his or her back. To identify the Bible forgiveness figures described on their backs, they must ask questions of their partners. Allow teens to continue this activity until everyone identifies the characters described on their backs.

Activities

Activity 1: Experiencing Sin and Alienation..................... 25 minutes

Supplies: • Bibles, one for each participant and group leader • one sheet of newsprint or posterboard for each group • pens or pencils, one for each participant and group leader • marking pens, highlighter pens • copies of ***Handout 2****, one for each participant and group leader • writing paper*

Divide a large sheet of newsprint or posterboard into columns. See the example at the top of the next page. Display this chart where everyone in your group is able to see it.

	Examples from real life	What emotions might these people be having?	What's happening to the relationships between these people?	
1				
2				
3				
4				
5				
6				
7				
8				

Give teens a minute or two to read the first statement on ***Handout 2***, and the short story printed below the statement. Ask how the statement and the story are related. Teens should see that the story is a real-life example that shows the truth of the statement. Now ask teens to think of situations from their own experience that illustrate unjust anger, and give them time to share these situations with one another. To get the sharing started, be prepared to offer an example of your own.

When you are sure that everyone understands how statement and story are related, ask teens to read the rest of the statements on the handout and write an example from real life for each statement. Have writing paper available for anyone who might need additional space for writing.

When everyone has finished, ask volunteers to share their examples, at least two for each statement. As each example is given, briefly summarize it on the newsprint or posterboard. Then, for each example, ask teens to answer the questions on the chart. Write answers as they are given. For emotions, teens will probably mention anger, hurt, frustration, sorrow. They are sure to see that the relationships involved are being damaged, but encourage them to be specific in saying how the relationships are being affected.

When everyone has had a chance to contribute to the chart, ask teens to use their Bibles to find these verses in the Book of Sirach: 1:22; 37:1; 37:7-8; 27:16; 22:27; 19:13-15; 5:9-10; 20:26. As each passage is found, ask a volunteer to read the passage out loud. During the reading, write the citation for the Scripture verse in the appropriate box in the first column of the chart.

From this exercise, teens should see that people have been experiencing the same problems with relationships for thousands of years.

Discussion Starter

- What words, phrases, expressions, and emotions were repeated for more than one example? (Highlight these as they are mentioned.)

Activity 2: Imagining Forgiveness and Reconciliation .... 10 minutes

*Supplies: • the chart prepared for **Activity 1** • marking pens*

To begin, fill in the first box in the last column of the chart. Write: How can this relationship be repaired? Ask teens to think of specific actions that the people involved could take to repair each damaged relationship.To help teens get started, be prepared to offer a suggestion of your own. Encourage everyone to participate.

Discussion Starter

- What words, phrases, expressions, and emotions were repeated for more than one example? (Highlight these as they are mentioned.)

Activity 3: Stand up and be counted! .... 15 minutes

*Supplies • copies of **Handout 3**, one for each participant and group leader • pens or pencils, one for each participant and group leader • four signs, one with each response written on it*

Ask teens to follow the directions at the top of the handout. While everyone is working, hang the signs in four different areas of the room. When everyone has finished, invite teens to share their opinions. Read the first statement and ask teens to move to the sign that agrees with their response to that statement. Then ask each teen to say briefly why he or she chose this response. Continue this process for all the statements. Encourage teens to discuss their experience.

Discussion Starters

- What do you think your responses say about your past experiences?
- What do your responses say about your beliefs?

Activity 4: What does it mean? .... *20 minutes*

Supplies • writing paper, one sheet for each participant and group leader • pens or pencils, one for each participant and group leader • one sheet of newsprint or posterboard for each group • marking pens

Divide a large sheet of newsprint or posterboard into four columns. For column headings, see the example below. Display this where everyone in your group is able to see it.

Give teens ten minutes to write their own definitions for these four words. When everyone has finished writing, encourage them to share what they have written. Begin by writing one of the definitions provided below and asking if anyone has a different idea to add.

Sin	Alienation	Forgiveness	Reconciliation
• deliberately doing something morally wrong • hurting oneself or others • making choices that prevent one's own growth or the growth of others • being self-centered	• separation that is painful • withdrawal of love or friendship	• showing compassion • renewing love and trust • freeing a person from blame and guilt • giving up resentment or a grudge	• putting things back together • bringing harmony back into a relationship • renewing love or friendship between those who have been alienated or separated

If, after everyone has had a chance to contribute to the chart, the definitions provided above have not been given, add them, asking for teens' reactions to each.

Break .... *10 minutes*

Presentation

Understanding What We Do and Say .... *10 minutes*

Supplies • copies of ***Handout 4****, one for each participant and group leader*

Because teens may not have celebrated the sacrament of Penance very often or very regularly, they may not be sure of what is involved in receiving the sacrament. Reassure them that we all feel nervous and anxious when we do not know what is expected of us or when we don't remember what to do and say. This handout should help to refresh their memories. Review the steps involved, allowing opportunities for teens to ask questions and express reactions. Sharing a reaction of your own may help teens to feel comfortable and help to get them started.

This review may also provide a good opportunity to allay fears teens may have about confessing sins to a priest. Stress that in the celebration of the sacrament of Penance, the priest is present as a representative of God and the Christian community. He is there to help the penitent —to listen and offer advice in a warm, friendly, loving way.

Sharing Our Stories .. *20 minutes*

Supplies • Bibles, one for each participant and group leader • pens or pencils, one for each participant and group leader • copies of ***Handout 5****, one for each participant and group leader*

Begin by pointing out that St. Luke's Gospel portrays Jesus as a compassionate savior who identifies with the poor and with sinners and outcasts. These stories from Luke's Gospel show the healing that comes with Jesus' forgiveness.

Ask teens to follow the directions on the handout and be prepared to discuss their written responses to the questions.

Activity 5: Prescription for Healing .... *30 minutes*

Supplies • one sheet of newsprint or posterboard for each group • marking pens, one for each group • copies of ***Handout 6****, one for each participant and group leader*

Divide a large sheet of newsprint or posterboard into columns. See example below. Display this chart where everyone in your group is able to see it.

Examples from the Media			
SINS		*VIRTUES*	
Pride		*Humility*	
Covetousness		*Generosity*	
Lust		*Chastity*	
Anger		*Gentleness*	
Gluttony		*Temperance*	
Envy		*Brotherly love*	
Sloth		*Diligence*	

Allow teens five to ten minutes of quiet time to fill in their handouts with examples from movies, television shows, songs, and events reported in newspapers and magazines to illustrate each of the sins listed. When everyone is finished writing, have teens share their examples by taking turns writing their examples on the chart. Allow time after each example is written for the teen to explain his or her choice, and for the others to express their reactions.

Repeat the process with examples of virtues.

Discussion starters

- For which was it more difficult to find examples—sin or virtue? Why do you think this might be true?
- In the examples given, what effect does sin have on relationships?
- In the examples given, what effect does virtue have on relationships?
- How do you think practicing Christian virtues would affect a person's life? A person's relationships?

Break .... *10 minutes*

Prayer Experiences

It would be ideal if teens could conclude this session by celebrating the sacrament of Penance. **Prayer Response 1** is a reconcilation service planned around the reception of the sacrament. **Prayer Response 2** is an option if a priest is not available.

Prayer Response 1: Reconciliation Service........................ 45 minutes

Supplies • copies of ***Handout*** *7, one for each priest, participant, and group leader • a tape or CD player • instrumental music to play softly during the individual confessions • Bibles, one for each participant and group leader • copies of the song book used in your parish or school, one for each participant and group leader*

To provide an opportunity for teens to celebrate the sacrament of Penance, you will need to contact a priest well in advance. Once you are sure a priest will be available, decide with him where the celebration will take place and what arrangements will need to be made for space for group seating, places for individual confessions, and additional priests if yours is a large group.

Enourage teens to select an opening and a closing song from among the songs that they are familiar with. They can select Scripture readings from among those that they worked with during this session or from these: Matthew 5:1-10; Matthew 22:36-39; Mark 11:25; Ephesians 4:25-32; 1 John 4:7-10. Ask volunteers to prepare the chosen readings ahead of time.

Prayer Response 2: Forgive us as we forgive others........... 15 minutes

Supplies • a Bible • copies of ***Handout 8****, one for each participant and group leader • writing paper, one sheet for each participant and group leader • pens or pencils, one for each participant and group leader • a tape or CD player • soft instrumental music to play in the background • a small hibachi, ready for a small fire, or a personal-size paper shredder*

Ask for volunteers to serve as leaders and readers. If possible, allow time for them to prepare their parts ahead of time.

Prepare a prayer space by placing a Bible and the hibachi or paper shredder on a small table. If possible, add fresh or dried flowers and a table covering.

During the prayer response, participants will be asked to write confidential responses to an examination of conscience. When everyone has finished writing, have participants take turns giving you their papers so that you can put them, one by one, into the fire in the hibachi or into the paper shredder. After each person's sheet of paper has disappeared, bless the person by making the sign of the cross on his or her forehead.

Making a Difference

Media Watch

Supplies • copies of ***Handout 6****, one for each participant to take home*

Encourage teens to invite their families to work together to fill in this handout with examples from movies, television shows, songs, and events reported in newspapers and magazines to illustrate each of the sins and virtues. This exercise should provide an opportunity for family members to share and discuss their values and to make critical judgments about what is being presented by the media.

Bible Forgiveness Figures

I squandered my share of my father's property to see the world. When I was starving and miserable, I went home and asked for my father's forgiveness.
(Parable of the prodigal son—Luke 15:11-32)

When my younger son demanded his share of my property and went off to see the world, I waited for him to return. And when he did, I prepared a great celebration.
(Parable of the prodigal son—Luke 15: 11-32)

I can't understand it. My brother leaves home and squanders his share of our father's property. I stay home and work. And who gets the party? He does.
(Parable of the prodigal son—Luke 15:11-32)

I was tending my sheep, when I noticed that one of the one hundred was missing. It might seem foolish, but I left all my sheep to find the one who was lost.
(Parable of the lost sheep—Luke 15:3-7)

I'm so relieved. I lost one of my ten silver coins. But I swept my house and searched carefully until I found the coin that I had lost.
(Parable of the lost coin—Luke 15:8-10)

I almost didn't even get to see Jesus because I'm so short. But now he's coming to stay at my house. That's enough to make me want to change my ways. *(Jesus and Zacchaeus—Luke 19:1-10)*

When I saw Jesus at Simon's house, I was overwhelmed at being in his presence. When my tears fell on Jesus' feet, I dried them with my hair. After I anointed his feet, he forgave my sins and told me to go in peace.
(A sinful woman forgiven—Luke 7:36-50)

I was shocked. When I invited Jesus to share a meal at my house, a woman who is a known sinner approached Jesus, weeping and anointing his feet. But he didn't send her away. Instead he forgave her sins and gave me a lecture.
(A sinful woman forgiven—Luke 7:36-50)

The woman was guilty of adultery, and the law was clear—she should be stoned to death. But we asked Jesus what he would say, hoping he would contradict the law. What he said was strange—let anyone among you who is without sin cast the first stone.
(The woman caught in adultery—John 8:1-11)

I was so frightened. I knew the punishment for my sin. But the Pharisees took me to a man named Jesus and asked him what he would say about my sin. After Jesus spoke, no one would condemn me.
(The woman caught in adultery—John 8:1-11)

I was afraid for Jesus and for that poor woman. I knew the Pharisees were hoping to trap Jesus into saying something wrong. But after he spoke, there was nothing anyone could do—not even the Pharisees.
(The woman caught in adultery—John 8:1-11)

The two of us—we deserved what we were getting. But Jesus didn't do anything wrong and still they mocked him and crucified him. I couldn't believe what he said—Father, forgive them; for they do not know what they are doing.
(The crucifixion of Jesus—Luke 23:32-43)

Experiencing Sin and Alienation

1. *Unjust anger cannot be justified.*

Today my friends and I spent the day at the beach. I asked Kim to go with me. I really like her, and I thought she liked me. But Kim spent the whole day swimming and joking around with another guy. She even drove home with him.

When I got home, my little brother asked me to help him fix his train set. I really came down on him, yelling about how he's always breaking stuff and telling him to leave me alone. I knew he was almost ready to cry when he left my room.

Now that I've had some time to cool off, I know that I took my anger at Kim out on my little brother. Poor kid, he never knew what hit him.

Write your own example for each statement.

2. *...some friends are friends only in name.*

**3. *All counselors praise the counsel they give,*
*but some give counsel in their own interest.***

**4. *Whoever betrays secrets destroys confidence,*
*and will never find a congenial friend.***

**5. *Who will set a guard over my mouth,*
And an effective seal upon my lips,
so that I may not fall because of them,
*and my tongue may not destroy me?***

**6. *Question a friend, for often it is slander;*
*so do not believe everything you hear.***

**7. *Do not winnow in every wind,*
or follow every path.
Stand firm for what you know,
*and let your speech be consistent.***

**8. *A liar's way leads to disgrace,*
*and his shame is ever with him.***

Stand up and be counted!

Please read these statements and, for each, write the response that best expresses how you feel about that statement. Choose one of these responses for each statement:

Agree strongly Agree Disagree Disagree strongly

____________________ 1. Only God forgives completely.

____________________ 2. Apologies are just words.

____________________ 3. Often it is hard, or almost impossible, to forget that someone has hurt us.

____________________ 4. A heated argument clears the air.

____________________ 5. "Forgive and forget" is good advice.

____________________ 6. Reconciliation must start with the person who was hurt.

____________________ 7. There are times when people are too ashamed to admit their wrongdoing.

____________________ 8. Often it is hard to apologize to someone.

____________________ 9. There are few people you can trust.

____________________ 10. When people argue or lie, they don't think about the fact that their actions are sinful.

Understanding What We Do and Say

As you enter the confessional or the reconciliation room, the priest greets you.

↓

After you make the sign of the cross, the priest talks to you about God's forgiving love.

↓

Next, you tell the priest about your life and the times you have sinned. This is **confession**. The priest helps you look at your life situation. Then, with the priest's help, you determine ways to avoid sin and deepen your love for God and for all God's people.

↓

The priest then talks to you about a new direction, suggesting a way for you to make up for your sinfulness. This is not a punishment, but a help to avoid sin in the future. This is **satisfaction** for sin.

↓

The priest now asks you to tell God that you are sorry for your sins. You may use your own words, a Church prayer, or prayer similar to the one given here. This is an expression of **contrition.**

O my God, I am truly sorry for my sins.
I firmly intend, with your help, to make up for my sins and to live as Jesus did.

The priest then extends his hand over your head and says a prayer of forgiveness. Your answer is "Amen." This is **absolution**.

↓

The priest asks you to say a prayer of thanks. Again, you may use your own words or one of the following prayers.

God of love, you give new life. You have forgiven me. I thank you with all my heart.

Lord Jesus, you have set me free from my sins. I thank you and ask you to help me live as you did.

↓

Finally the priest wishes you the Lord's peace. Thank him as you leave.

Sharing Our Stories

Read these stories and write brief answers to the questions.

Luke 7:36-50

- What does the woman do to show that she is sorry for her sins?
- Do you think that Simon thinks of himself as a sinner? Why?
- What do you think Jesus means when he tells the woman to go in peace? Do you think going in peace includes avoiding sin? Why?

Luke 15:11-32

- What words does the younger son use to tell his father that he is sorry for his actions?
- Does the older son think of himself as a sinner? Why?
- Are you aware of a similar situation in your family or in another family you know? If so, please describe it briefly.
- What would each person in this story need to do to contribute to the healing of the family?

Luke 19:1-10

- How does Zacchaeus respond to Jesus?
- Did the people who grumbled about Jesus' decision to stay with Zacchaeus think of themselves as sinners? Why?
- How would Zacchaeus' promises bring healing to his life?

John 8:1-11

- What does this story tell us about judging others?
- What does the woman need to do to bring healing to her life?

A Prescription for Healing

Examples from the Media			
Sins		Virtues	
Pride		***Humility***	
Covetousness		***Generosity***	
Lust		***Chastity***	
Anger		***Gentleness***	
Gluttony		***Temperance***	
Envy		***Brotherly love***	
Sloth		***Diligence***	

Reconciliation Service

Greeting

The presider welcomes all, introduces himself and any other priests who are participating, and explains what the sacrament of Penance can mean to all who receive it.

Opening Song

Opening Prayer

All: Jesus, you came so that we might be reconciled with God our Father and with one another. Give us the courage and strength to live as you did.

Scripture Readings

Homily

Priest: Let us pause now and reflect on how we have failed during the past weeks.

Examination of Conscience

Reflect on your answers to these questions as preparation for your confession.

- Do I treat people with kindness—my parents, brothers and sisters, friends, teachers?
- Am I kind only to people who do what I want them to?
- Do I hurt others intentionally—by mocking them, putting them down, embarrassing them?
- Do I abuse the bodies of others for my own gratification?
- Do I abuse my own body by misusing drugs or alcohol?
- Do I respect authority?
- Am I willing to listen to my parents and teachers?
- Do I think that I should always be able to do things my way?
- Am I honest with myself and others?
- Do I shoplift and excuse myself by saying that everyone is doing it?
- Do I cheat in my school work and excuse myself by saying that everyone is doing it?
- Do I make an honest effort to pray—to talk and listen to God?
- Do I participate in Sunday Liturgy?
- Do I truly try to make God, his word, and the Church a part of my life?

Act of Repentance

Priest: Let us pray together for God's forgiveness and his help to change our lives.

To each statement, all respond:
Forgive me, God, and help me change.

There have been times in my life when I unkind to others.

There have been times in my life when I was dishonest, deliberately cheating and shirking my responsibilities.

There have been times in my life when I turned from God, making myself number one.

All: God, help me to know myself. Give me the courage to admit my sins. I know that I have often chosen to do wrong. I am sorry for my sins. Please forgive me. I believe that your constant love makes it possible for me to change my life. That's why I pray...

All join in praying the Our Father.
A time for private confessions follows. When all have finished, the presider offers a blessing and invites everyone to join in singing.

Closing Song

Forgive us as we forgive others

Form a circle around the table and prepare for prayer by breathing deeply and evenly and quieting your body and mind.

Leader 1: *(Begins with the sign of the cross)* Dear God, as followers of Jesus, we gather to celebrate the forgiveness and reconciliation that he made possible. We ask your guidance and your grace as we reflect on our lives and our relationships with others and with you.

Reader: A reading from the Gospel of St. Matthew (*Reads Matthew 6:5-15, and ends by announcing:* The Gospel of the Lord)

All: Praise to you, Lord Jesus Christ.

Examination of Conscience

Leader 2: *Our Father, who art in heaven, hallowed be your name; your kingdom come; your will be done on earth as it is in heaven.*

Leader 3: For the times we have ignored you, our God, Creator of all that is good, we ask...

To each petition, all respond:
Forgive us now and help us to do your will.

For allowing other persons and things to take your place in our hearts and minds, we ask...

For paying attention to false heroes, people whose values are contrary to those of Jesus, we ask...

For the times we have misused and abused your holy name, we ask...

For failing to praise and thank you for all that you have given us, we ask...

For taking credit for your action in our lives and for thinking of ourselves as little gods, we ask...

For the times we failed to participate at Mass, we ask...

For the times we could have and should have spent in prayer, we ask...

For the times we could have and should have encouraged our friends to pray, we ask...

Leader 2: *Give us this day our daily bread; and forgive us our trespasses as we forgive those who trespass against us; and lead us not into temptation, but deliver us from evil.*

Leader 4: For the times we chose to ignore our parents and others in authority, we ask...

To each petition, all respond:
Forgive us as we forgive others.

For speaking or acting disrespectfully toward our parents and others in authority, we ask...

For the times we failed to follow our parents' good example, we ask...

For the times we failed to set a good example for our younger brothers and sisters, we ask...

For the times we hurt others, we ask...

For the times we failed to reach out to others and to share generously, we ask...

For the times we gossiped and damaged someone's reputation, we ask...

For the times we excluded others from our groups, we ask...

For taking what does not belong to us—things, homework answers, credit for what we did not accomplish—we ask...

For damaging or misusing property that does not belong to us, we ask...

For telling lies and half-truths about others, we ask...

For allowing others to take the blame for our misdeeds, we ask...

For wanting more than we truly need, we ask...

For failing to enourage others to respect people and property, we ask...

As a confidential response to this examination of conscience, write the sins you are most sorry for and a statement or prayer promising God that you will try to avoid these sins in the future. Take turns handing your papers to the group leader who will either burn the papers in a hibachi or feed them into a paper shredder.

Closing Prayer: We thank and praise you, O God. And we ask you to be with us as we try to live in peace. Amen.